One Day on the
Streets of Mumbai

A Tale of a Young Man
from Midnight to Midnight

Sandesh Shinde

PublishAmerica
Baltimore

ISBN: 978-1-4489-9838-8
PUBLISHED BY PUBLISHAMERICA, LLLP
www.publishamerica.com
Baltimore

Printed in the United States of America

One Day on the Streets of Mumbai

*A Tale of a Young Man
from Midnight to Midnight*

FOREWORD

MUMBAI IS THE CITY WHICH NEVER SLEEPS.
OBVIOUSLY, IT NEVER WAKES UP.
IT IS NOT THE CITY. IT IS A LIFE.
EVERYONE IN THIS CITY HAS A STORY TO TELL, A SAGA
TO SHARE AND A LIFE TO CHERISH.

THERE ARE A FORTUNATE FEW WHO MANAGE TO GET EVERYTHING THEY WISH BUT 99% ARE ON THE OTHER SIDE WHO SLEEP WITH A DREAM IN THEIR EYES AND WAKE UP WITH DEARTH SERVED TO THEM.

THIS IS A STORY OF YOUNG MAN WRITTEN IN A NARRATIVE POETIC FORMAT DEPICTING WHAT COMES BEFORE HIM DURING THE 24 HOURS OF HIS SOJOURN IN THIS CITY. IT IS A TRUE STORY.

THE YOUNG MAN IN THIS STORY HAS RECEIVED A PHONE CALL FROM HIS LOVE. HE IS GOING TO MEET HER IN THE EVENING. THE STORY REVEALS THE TRAUMA UNDERWENT BY HIM IN SEARCH OF HIS LOVE.

SINCE THE STORY CONTAINS CERTAIN REALITIES WHICH ARE NOT ADVISABLE TO BE DISCLOSED CITING THE NAMES ETC., AN EFFORT HAS BEEN MADE TO NARRATE IT AS IF THE STORY OF MINE. THE FEELINGS OF THE YOUNG MAN ARE WITH REFERENCE TO THE INDIAN CONTEXTS AND HAVE NO RESEMBLANCE TO PERSPECTIVE OF ANY COMMON INDIAN.

*

At a distant slums, not far off from my bedroom,
A barking dog is alarming the 'goodnight' to all.
I will also have to try closing my eyes
By pulling the blanket
From a few holes of which
Fresh humidity can be breathed in
And stars and the stones in the sky
Can be counted,
Irrespective of the fact that
Some of them are already present with me,
To be there till I breath the last,
Scattered in the way they
Wanted at the time of my birth,
Fixing their places in my *kundali*.

*

God knows as to why various
Rituals and rites are performed
To pacify them and minimize the
Side effects of their wrong positions
Despite the fact that they are never
Going to change their positions in the kundali.

*

Many of such paradoxes have no answers.
Why to try and find out one
Particularly when it is not going to
Change the fate—either of myself
Or the rest of the world.
Have to try and sleep.
The dog might bark again and I will be unable to sleep whole night.
I have to do a lot of things in the dreams.
Have to win the jackpot,
Have to take her to the *Taj* for the first time,
Kiss her in the dark niche of the staircase,
Leading to the terrace.
Show her the sky and the stars and promise her
To buy one *BHK* in the city,
On lines with almost every alternate
Person, born in the city
Incapacitated by the holes in his wallet,
Thinks and feels honored by himself
If he manages somehow a roof
Around the city
Probably on the outskirts of it.

*

So many dreams….
So many.
Perhaps one night is not enough to dream them all.
In the next 3-4 hours only one thing has to be done,
Live for myself.

*

How can I live if I sleep like others?
The time has come to live
Suppressing illusions and the arousals
Holding the desires hard in hand
So as to avoid spillage thereof.
Therefore the eyes are closed,
But the brain and the soul are still conscious.

*

Some might have placed their dreams under the pillow
Before entering the dark in the inner side of the eyelids.
I pushed her fainted photo after having a last look at it
Wishing her a good night.
The nights were never good for me, the days either.

*

The window is to be closed.
It was a carved window.
Then a tinted one followed by a single and a double window.
The window has remained window.
A permeable partition,
Between the two worlds.

*

I changed it.
So many times.
The other side is unchanged.
Yet.

*

One day I will check how it looks inside.
From the other side of window.

*

But now the time has come to close it anyway.
A creeper is hanging from above.
A few flowers and buds on it.
A ray is coming across the pane.
Soft breeze is coming in
Bringing in a distant siren of a passing train
At a mile away,

*

The street has closed its business
Of carrying the loads on its chest.
Human loads, mechanical loads, normal loads,
Payloads, loads, loads and loads on loads.
The dirty beggar at the right hand side streetlight pole,
Must have collected the donations given in inhuman manner.
The roads bustling with the run and jerks of
The agility and ambitions clashing with each other
Are slowly coming to a minor lull..

*

There is no time to dream.
There is no time to nurture the existing ones.
The dreams are broken before dreaming of, every moment.
Completing hundreds and thousands of permutation
And combinations, calculations and speculations,
The tired city has entered into an uneasy paradigm.

*

The dirty beggar has completed his business
And returned to his paraphernalia.
The street has unloaded every load.
The sirens have stopped piercing the sky.
The breeze has changed the smell.
The ray in the window has vanished after changing the side.
The flowers of the morning have drooped.
The buds are waiting for the dawn to blossom.
The creeper looks gloomy and dark.
The window is closed.
Through the rifts and crevices of the old window,
The barking of the street dogs is heard.
It is not going to stop whole night.
How to bring someone in the dream?
Dreams have no definition.
It is a reality on the other side of the window.
To dream it is a task and it is too taxing.
Let me close the eyes to face the nightmares.

*

Perhaps, I will sleep.
But the Gods and parents behind the dried garlands
Might not sleep keeping an eye on me for my well being.

*

After 2 years or so, she has ranged up asking me
To come at the same spot where we had met last
And she left me asking me to do something for our future
And promised to meet me again.

*

Since then I have tried all my best to uplift myself
With the sole degree and rigorous efforts,
Pains, & empty stomach even without a *wada-pav*
Which fills the pit below the diaphragm of
Half of the Mumbai.

*

Since then I have not met her.
She has not met me.
I thought she will never come back to my life.
She doesn't know I am working somewhere,
Earning fair enough to meet both ends meet.
And with her income brought together,
We could certainly live a better life leaving behind the loneliness
And the dearth and the plight.
Forever.

*

But I know,
I know even if I bring
All the stars and the moon
And put them in her hands
And even if I take
All the oceans in my stride
And squeeze them to a drop,
She won't believe it could be me
Who, besides dreaming her
And loving her
Could do anything else.

I know even if I bend the
Rainbow and sprinkle
The colors of it
On her face,
And even if I pluck my heart
And place it before her
In the test of my love
She won't believe as to how
I could do such a miracle
For the sake of her love.

*

I know she won't believe
Me and my love.
The desires in my eyes
And the glow.
Still I will love her
Till the end of me,
Lest her change her mind
And think to follow after I show her my current month's pay slip.

*

I must sleep now.
It is raining out there.
The trains may be late tomorrow and therefore I must reach the station
early
To catch the *8.57 CCG fast.*

*

The same train, leaning out of which
I used to look at her everyday till the train crossed the platform

And the platform looked like a collage of colors
Waiting for the *9.10 CCG fast.*

*

I am unable to describe all those moments
From the time we first met at the same spot where
I am once again meeting her today at her call.
I have preserved those moments for myself.
Never crossing the corporeal limits,
The love lasted for 8 years
And after a break of 2 years or so
There will a pledge today not to depart again.
Hitherto the affair has remained unknown to the rest of the world.
The friend who knew it has passed away
A week before by the cardiac arrest.
I guess he was also in love with someone
Who took his heart leaving behind the attack for him.

*

When she comes, I will show her
Each and every alphabet
Of her letters to me,
Preserved as a history
Of mine that would be written
On my tomb.
But I cannot show her
The tears flown down,
The sleepless nights,
The hallucinations,
The emotions
And
The desires,
I suppressed

And
The probable
Offspring,
Flown into the gutters,
Anticipating her,
And finding her womb.

*

Anyway, I have to rush to the station
To push myself inside the womb of train full of
Similarly placed people of smaller and/or no Gods.

*

It is 8.57 by now and the train is about to start.
Once again it will pass through the stations halting at a few
And leaving behind many.

*

Fast running trees and *nallahs*—luckily I do not find
My reflection therein though the vegetables grown on its water
On the either sides of them are served to almost every alternate,
Make me feel that I am on the right track
Even though the train is running behind its schedule
By a margin of 20 minutes.

*

Fortunately, the cell is on the silent mode.
At least till I come out of the train and look at the missed calls,
There won't be any reminding executives
Seeking immediate payment of the *EMIs* to avoid the penalties
And the interests

And those of them insisting for the payment today itself.
I just wonder as to how the EMIs once skipped for any reason
Slowly reach the number of EMIs payable
More than the actually paid ones.

*

And there is a corpse, half cut, lying on the outer side of the track.
Some crows are piercing their beaks as fast as they can
To get maximum of their share of flesh through the bones,
Amongst the thousands of the flies hovering over it.
Since the crows have already touched the body, is there
Any need of *pind dan* required to be performed as a routine
At the end of *13th*?
May the soul rest in peace. I murmured.
Lest such a scene shall not come in anyone's life including me.

*

The train is leaving stations one after another and I am
Coloring the imagination as to what could happen in the
Evening when she comes to meet me, by stretching spectrum too far,
Even beyond my capacity to correlate myself with her in the changed
scenario.

*

I still remember
The paper that
Turned pink

And
Alphabets as petals,
Of her letter
I possess.
And I believe,
Perhaps,
She has palms
Made of roses.

*

The letter given by her, the last one,
Is still in my pocket carefully preserved,
Though needs some restoration
Which I might get in the evening
In redemption of all my best deeds and the fidelity
Ever since she left me last.

*

The whole day now is to be spent
With the fast shifting paradigms amongst the absurdities.
The heap of files, the chaos,
The benchmarks, the distant increment, uncertain promotions,
Application for short loan
Pending the application for long loan
Pending GPF withdrawal, muster, roster
And so on and so forth.........
How could I survive in the jungle full of such carnivorous entities?

*

But I am alive, survived of all the hurdles and attacks
Though the desires were never fulfilled
As those of the parallel lines of the track,

Keeping constant distance between them,
Never meet each other except the at the point where they change the line,
Again keeping the equal distance between them and
Enter into new paradigm,
Where the desires of others clash along with other entities.
I being the one line and everything else desired and dreamt as the other one.

*

The train is crossing the bridge on the *mithi river*
Which now has become a nallah meeting the *Mahim creek*.
I believe one of my friends who drowned on *26th July*
Must be still there screaming for the help.
Perhaps, when *MCGM* completes widening of the river,
Most likely before this monsoon itself, it might get the remains of my friend.
Meanwhile, I must go his parents to ask them if they needed any help,
As a part of my social duty.

*

Should I get down at *Dadar* to get some gift for her?
No, I think not. She may not like it.
Once she had asked me not to bring any gifts for her.
Maybe because she knew the size of my wallet
Or she was much confident of my poor choices coupled with the
idiosyncrasy.

*

I know I cannot take the stars in my stride
To sprinkle on her and make her pride.
I cannot give her gifts more than a kiss,
Do I deserve to love her, or am I amiss?

*

I know I cannot build a Taj for her
In the token my love to her.
Therefore, I wish
She lives long and dies after me.
If my prayer is accepted, she will die after me.
At least one burden is removed from the head.

*

Who says everyone has his own sky above his head
And that the sky is the limit
And by and for some, even the sky is not the limit?
There are burdens,
There are satellites,
There are stellar objects
On and over the head of each and everyone.
It is said that the heavens are there in the deep sky.
And the black holes as well.
Nobody has ever returned to describe them yet
Maybe because the heavens are illusions
And the black holes the reality.
Time stops there.
Just like the life stops with the last breath,
Leaving everyone else breathless for a few moments.
In a manner nothing less than the position in the train compartment.
People are so close to each other
That one might get merged into another.
One can easily identify brand and the quantity
Of the overnight consumption of every other person
Simply from the sweat emanating from the body
Burning the hair in the nostrils.

*

Some are entering the telephone number
Of the erectile dysfunction clinic in their cell phones
While some are testing their abilities
By adjusting against the back of another.
Some are etching their bases
Looking at the details of the piles clinic
Pasted unauthorized on the inner side of the compartment
While some have engaged themselves
In the *Mandir* and the *Masjid* looking forward for the better option,
Separated by a very thin line of the religious identities.
Some are looking forward for the part time job ads.
Some are busy looking forward for financiers.
And some looking outside the window into the nil
Connecting themselves with the Gods in the heaven
Asking them to shower some luck onto them
So that the *sensex* rises at least to such an extent
That brings back the ornaments of wife back home
And that the house is also saved from mortgage.
All possible solutions for all problems of India in a single train compartment-
A solution cubicle.

*

The *sensex* will decide the rush in the return journey.
If it is high, there will be rush in the trains
And if it falls, the trains will be fairly empty.
At least there will be some space between the noses of two
People so that they could breath independently.
One building bifurcates the people
Of the city,
With a clear demarcation as to who will sleep peacefully tonight
And who will toil through the night as a result of the color of the triangles
Under some alphabetical combinations called *scrip*.

*

It is apprehended that one day
Half of the city will receive a severe heart attack
And the remainder will come to a standstill with the shock
If the recession continues collapsing the indices.
Perhaps, then there won't be takers for the mansions
And the slums might touch the skies above their roofs.
Perhaps, tsunami could be a better option.
At least half would survive
Even if half are drowned in the *Arabian Sea*.
The rhetoric of removing outsiders will be reduced
Proportionate to the percentage of survivors.
Some statues will be uprooted and flow down the gutters.
This will wide open new opportunities
For the some to continue baking their breads-
A business provided by the great forefathers of the country and the
land
To the political siblings of theirs
While re-establishing their statues.
The crow sitting on the head of Gandhi
Hears him crying, sees him weeping
But we do not listen the crow
Till the 365th day when it is needed
To touch the *pind*.
Unless it touches offering,
The fast can not be broken.
It is called by invitation.
By one and all.
After all everyone has a stomach.
No matter, the father has died.

*

A bridge is being built
Between some slum dogs at one end
And the millionaires on the other,
With a restriction of toll
So that none of the slum dogs
Could ever have a oceanic ride
Towards the millionaires.
A few of the further segments
Are also proposed to be built
In furtherance of widening
Distance between two people-
One who do not afford a wada pav to fill their stomach
And the other who start their day in *Mc'donald's.*
I must save my paraphernalia.
Maybe one day I will cross the sea link
On my own.

*

To break my day dream,
There are *bhajan mandalis* in the compartment
Singing *Shirdiwale Sai Baba* which reminds me that today is Thursday.
I do not know whether the *Sai Baba* will respond to the *Bhajans* or not.
But I believe He is not dead.
He must have gone to the deep in Himalayas.
He will come back.
Yes, certainly.
He has to.
Otherwise both the claimants of his
Will leave no one to take care of his *Darbar.*
I wish He reincarnates in *Ayodhya.*
Once I had been to *Shirdi*
Along with Jennie.

In fact she had taken me there
To say sorry to him
And get forgiven for all her sins
She had committed while and after luring the customers.
She was a bargirl.

*

I don not know what and where she is now a days.
But I remember, once while returning from her job,
Her *auto* was stopped by some hooligans and they wanted to pull her
out.
Fortunately, I happened to be there returning from *Samrat* with my
friends and rescued Her of a probable gang rape.

*

Jennie—a deserted wife of a *Dubai* returned driver
Was making both the ends meet by serving in a *dance bar*.
She needed a support.
Particularly after the incidence.
I extended it.
Thereafter so many of my nights passed in her bed.
She needed it.
I provided it.
But I want to forget all these things.
I know she had helped me a lot in my days of plight.
Had she not given me money,
I could not start my degree course in Mumbai University
Under distance learning programme.
The degree of B.A. has brought me up to the current position.
Maybe I will have to pay her back the debts.
One of my eyes always search for her.
I have visited almost every likely place
Where there was any chance of getting her.

Unfortunately, I do not have mechanism to check her whereabouts
Amongst millions of people living like bees in the hive.
I remember her face but she may not identify me now
I have undergone so many changes.
Hope she might have got someone and married.
At least I wish so.

*

Maybe she will never come across me.
But the cross she had got tattooed on my right hand under the thumb
Will remain forever with me in a token of the memories spent with her
Outside the bed and under the suns.
She had got the cross on my hand against my will.
I told her that I was Hindu
And that tattooing signs of any other religion was forbidden for me.
She did not listen.
I was helpless.
I succumbed to her plea that even being Hindu
I had been in the *Mt. Merry Church* with her
Offered candles and prayed there for the well being of all of us.
Unwillingly, two lines perpendicular to each other
Were inscribed in a painful manner.

*

I did not believe the power of these lines
Till I was saved of being killed in the *Hindu-Muslim* riots in Mumbai.
Both the communities considered me to be either an already
endangered species
Or a harmless entity
Or an alien
Who looked like a Hindu
But spoke fluent Hindi.
Before asking my name to decide my fate, luckily

They looked at my hand and left me unhurt.
Even some of Jennie's friends and relatives asked me to marry her
Thinking that I was a Christian.

*

The train is stopping now at the destination.
The passengers will repeat the same exercise of jumping over each
other
To get out of it in the same manner what they had done while getting
in.
The empty station is filled again with hundred of men and women
Walking briskly towards their individual destinations
Like the ants pouring out of a broken anthill,
Trying to reach before everyone else
And soon the station will be empty once again till the next
Train arrives.

*

Avoiding the jerks of fellow passengers,
Trying to hold myself perpendicular on the feet,
Railing across the stream of entire population of the city
Accumulated in a single place,
I am pushing myself forward
Towards the Office through a tunnel called underground passage,
Filled with human stink.
If everyone else is so stinky, so am I for the others.
Nobody hates anyone else here like the passengers of Noah's Boat.
It is the essence of life.
Everyone is under a compulsion to bear the every alternate person-
Willingly or unwillingly.
It is not a matter at all.

*

These living domains travel in same direction-
Once in the morning and then in the evening.
If a single domain collapses, the entire row comes to an end.
But the living domains in this city hold each other.
Taking left and then right and then left,
Somehow I am making my way to the other end of the underground
Through the Gods employed on the walls to protect them from spits
of *Gutka*.
The Gods on the natural spittoons of the city.
All Gods,
No exemption.
The miracle of the metropolitan city.
Nowhere on this third rock from the sun is there any place
Having a conglomeration of the Gods of all religion.
The Gods worshipped at the foot,
The Gods before whom the heads are bowed
Are finding their placements at the foot.
How will these Gods, so employed will solve my problems?
How are those, pasted on the walls are going to listen to anybody
Amongst the cacophony and chaos,
Saving themselves from the sprinkles of the Gutka?

*

Will she come today?
What will she ask?
What will she decide?
Or will she lead me to another desertion with a promise to meet again
Or conclude never to meet again?

*

Thousands of thoughts,
Thoughts after thoughts,
Wishful thoughts,
Unwanted thoughts,
Pessimistic thoughts,
Optimistic thoughts.

*

Will she take my hand in her hands
Or will she straight away lend her head on my shoulder?
Perhaps she might weep seeing me.
Last time I had wept when she left.
Maybe she will repent on her act.
Thousands of thoughts entering my head.
Every thought is biting like an ant.
I am afraid lest the brain might burst out of the skull
And scatter on the street.
It is unnecessary to think ten thousand time on anything.
It is said that out of the ten thousand thoughts encircling anything,
Any one of them is correct and the rest of 9999 are futile.
In fact to find out the correct one,
Efforts are required to make for 9999 times.

Till the correct thought is caught, correct moment to act on it lapses.
Such moment is yet to come to my life. Loosing it is just another thing.
However, the thoughts have not yet ceased to come.

*

Have taken a left leading towards Office.
What am I going to do in the Office
Other than repeating the same story?
If I absent today, is the heaven going to fall?
At the most, the steno of the boss will place her eyes on the doors
Till the lunch time expecting me to come for a half day.
Perhaps she might skip her lunch.
It is not that we feed each other.
Her digestive system doesn't work unless she sees my face.
She might prefer acidity to dysentery today.
Better I do not go to Office today.

*

For two years, she has kept me on her glances.
It is flirting not amounting to debauchery., I suppose.
And after all, I have also provided meaning to her beauty by the return
glances.
God knows as to how I am entangled in her, a little.
But I must forget her.
Forever.
At least from today.
She takes dictation.
In the evening I am going to take dictation from my love.
Big orders in shorthand.
May be the final orders
Or the beginning of unending end, one step ahead.

From this footpath, hundreds of gamblers might have headed
To pull the sensex,
Lift the sensex
And returned home from the same footpath,
Having lost everything of the paraphernalia,
Except the last belonging—the train pass.
Some of them have stories like fairy tales,
Needed to be listened by one and all.
But the fairy tales are fairy tales and those seldom are the realities for others.

I don't understand as to why everyone is running
To leave every other behind him
With a permanent question mark on everyone's face
And unbearable loads on the head,
Though invisible.

On the other side of the road,
A few factories have been set up to produce future *Sachins*.
Perhaps in a short while,
There wont be any number 2 in the Indian Cricket Team.
Invincible optimism of the parents.
What else?
These boys will directly become youth
Bypassing the natural phase of adolescence.
These buds will never blossom.
They will enter the productive phase of seeds.
Childhood in the peril.
Nothing less than that of mine in other way.
I still remember the day on which we fell short of 10 *paise*

To get a ticket for entry in *Rani Baug*.
The gatekeeper had chased us away
Like the man on the counter of the sweetshop sway away the flies.

*

I will buy a book for her to give her as a gift or a present in token my
love to her.
Which book should I take?
No strains are required to be given on the brain cells
While on this footpath.
Just decide and the book and it is in your hands.
If you pick up Gandhi's My experiments With Truth
The dust will fall on the speeches of Adolph Hitler
And under him there is Stalin smothered for so many days.
Everything on sale.
What does she like?
Poems or Prose?
I do not remember properly.
But I remember I had sung a few of my collections for her.
I do not know whether she liked them or not.
Maybe she might not have understood them
Or may be I could not understand whether she liked them or not.

*

I think in a normal way as that any other *Hindu*.
I don't know how a girl from Hindu father and Christian mother thinks.
She is a cross breed.

Therefore, I am always in a crux.
Anyway, as she has fallen in love with me,
She will certainly understand my emotions and arousals.
Otherwise, there will be little option left than to take her to *Khajuraho*.
But before that I will endorse her love by taking oath before the Taj.

*

Instead of giving her book,
Is it not an extraordinary idea to present her my poems?
At least she will not throw them on my face.
Decided.
I will take a printout from the cybercafé.
Of course, some of the poems of the collection have lost the relevance.
Those are required to be deleted.
Forever.
Change of the relevance has magnified the meanings thereof.
In some cases the relevance is distorted.
Maybe that she might take different meanings out of them
If not deleted or altered, suited to the contemporary position.
Just placing the pen on the paper does not give birth to poems.
It takes the ink of emotions.
The emotions have long been killed—
sometimes by myself in an effort to overcome the plight and the dearth.
Now the poems come to the front side of the brain
And get lost from the other side of it.
I place no effort to hold them.
I have no courage either to do so.
The emotions are lost in this city
Like the ship dragged haphazardly in the storms having no shore for it
to land.
Perhaps, dovetailing the remnants of a few feelings,
A novel could take a shape.

*

Whenever my brain will be opened,
In the routines of post mortem,
You will find signs of abnormal death.
A large section of it would be filled with
Anguish,
Distress,
Pains,
Despair,
Destitute.
Remainder would be lethargic replica of mine.
No place for emotions.
But she has hands of roses.
The paper has
Turned pink
And
Alphabets as petals,
Of her letter
I possess.

*

The love has anesthetic effect.
It numbs the brain and the heart
And intoxicates the feelings.
Have you ever seen anyone fallen in love
Walking straight and in normal course?
No one can do so if he or she is in real love.

*

I feel, all the milestones have been achieved by the great people
Because at one point or the other they must have been in love with
someone.

Those succeeded built the Tajs
And those failed, the concentration camps,
Distinguishing between loved and getting loved.

*

The love makes everything look great.
Not only the Taj, but everything else.
But it doesn't remain so nice for all the times.
The world around those who get it becomes beautiful
But at the same time it looks mutilated when someone departs from
someone.

*

Whenever I see a falling star
Stretching a streak behind it,
I feel the pains in my inner heart
And stab on the outer a bit.
Whenever I see golden dusk
Calling the love to meet again,
I close my eyes filled with tears
and roll them down releasing pain.
Whenever I see a fallen rose,
Mutilated and torn apart,
I lift it in my shivering hands
Wishing her back, not to depart.

*

In the cyber café at the corner of the street
Printout have been taken of the poems,
Composed in the dilemma,
And going to be presented to another dilemma.

*

The dilemma of to be or not to be
Is not a dilemma to me.
How to be is a question,
Unresolved till now.
Leading to another dilemma-
Why to be?

*

The poems have come out of this dilemma.
Some of them are now cut.,
Some are crossed to be forgotten forever,
Some are reworded.
This has lead to a great mess now.
Only one identifiable thing has remained
And it is my name under each of them.
The only identity remaining with me coupled with my signature,
My name.
The signature has no value even on my own pay-in slips.
I wonder as to how I am going to endorse it on her heart.

*

Never understood the depth of her heart.
Had I been empowered to enter her heart,
At least I would have known the niche where I am placed,
If at all I am there till the moment.
As she has called me herself,
She must have removed the dust accumulated on me
And must be remembering that she herself has placed me there.

*

Take my heart.
It is for you.
But don't break it,
For you might rue.
It will show you,
you on the walls
And the tubes
And the valves.
There are lines
Showing the cuts.
Given by you
On either crusts.
It is pumping
In the name of you.
Blood is sparkling
Like dew.
Please go deep
There is a niche,
Carved for you
Painted rich.
Be there,
Forever,
even if I do not find any place
In the heart of yours.

*

One unidentifiable fear of loosing the self penetrates through the spine chord.
Unnecessarily and unwarrantedly.
Such fear had penetrated me twice before in my lifetime.
Once on 26th July and then on *26th November.*
On both these days everyone had been under the threat of being killed.

The skies had taken the charge of the city with torrential rains in the
first incidence
And on the second time,
The death emerged out of the *Arabian Sea* in the form of terrorists attack.
Both had H_2O connection.
Efforts were made earlier also by the contractors of religious identities
To burn the whole city into ashes.
But the bids have been foiled by larger half of the citizens.
The bombs also couldn't tear the life apart.
Because, every time other person was at peril
And everyone was in the business of rescuing himself.

*

But today it could be a day to lose the self.
If she denies my amour, the love,
There will be no ray of hope
Even when the sun is going to be there
For another some million years.

*

It is alright to fall in love
But it is deadly to fall short of it or beyond,
At least for a hyper sensitive person like me.
I shouldn't have loved her.
There is no time to live here,
There is no time to die here,
From where shall one bring the time to love and the wait for it?
The life can not be halted,
It should not halt for any reason either,
Big or small.
Life is an endeavor
To leave no margin
Between two breaths.

But she—the specimen chapter of incomplete biology
Didn't understand this.

*

I think the life is left with the those crows
Sitting on the roofs of the British age buildings,
The pigeons finding niche in the olden houses
And the sparrows around the slums.
May be she is thinking that I am a crow.
Like a crow atop a temple.
Black.
She has to be told that
I am destined different—
A white crow.
Like a few others.
The black crows do not accept me.
Because,
I am not black.
Like them.

*

And there are parrots either
Fairly distant in complexion as that of mine,
Caged by the man sitting under that banyan tree,
Telling the future to people who have no future.
One of them is sitting there on the other side of the road.
May I ask him the line up of my stars for me tonight?
Will he tell the truth
Or the parrot will die in place of me seeing my future?
Wish it doesn't.

*

The parrot will take the exact card out of the 12,
Once my name enters its ears.
My star sign card.
The man will, without any expressions on his face,
Tell me my printed future.
It is a surprise.
All the millions of people divided into 12.
Everyone belonging to any one of those cards
And not the least, every twelfth man has same future
And same heavenly array of the stars.
Today, Tomorrow and every day thereafter.
Future doesn't change here, unless the man alters the words.
He is almighty.
In this city one can touch any tree on which a photo frame of his Gods
is hanging and go ahead on his business.
There is no need to go to temples, churches, mosques.
Everything is on the roads.
Gods on the roads.
Anyone before going to the wine shop can touch anyone of these,
Say sorry for the misdeed he is going to perform
And rest assured that someone is there to take care of all his wrongs.
There is no religious barrier.
All Gods for all people of lesser and greater Gods.
Metropolitan humanity, metropolitan worship.

*

There is a cow tied up to the tree
And a woman is sitting at its feet.
Almost every alternate person is touching it.
Some of them are feeding grass by buying from that woman.
I touched the cow in token of touching *33 crore Gods* at once.

Cow is better option than the parrot and the tarots.
At least no linking agent for and on behalf heavenly figures will say anything
To further aggravate the situation.

*

It looks that the *market* will remain unstable today.
Someone was telling in the train.
Others were optimistic and nullifying his statements and theories.
There was a solar eclipse of the century in the recent past.
It is said that the eclipse is going to bring bad days for all.
The television channels are screaming about the anti-human
repercussions of the eclipse by giving the historic examples of the
holocaust
Cased by the similar eclipses in the past,
With help of the rhetoric
emanating from the self proclaimed damage control contractors
Of the firmamental disaster,
Misleading everybody
Including those literates who have studied the reasons of the eclipse
In the 4th standard text books.

*

It is the city where anything normal
Can take a shape of absolute abnormality.
Once, *Lord Ganapati* had forgotten the capillary action force theory
And drank almost every drop of milk in the dairies.
By the time the milk in the city ended,

There were news that the Ganapati was employed in the same business
Across the U.S.

*

Next of similar eclipse is going to happen 123 years later.
Nobody, at least from this generation is destined to have a chance to
see it.
Even this time, it was impossible to get a chance
To see the heavenly miracle once read in the text books.
Many a things of the text books have remained there only.
How the invisible eclipse is going to affect the waggling creators under
it?
How the rays or no rays emanating out of it are going to affect the star
signs
The stars and their array in the kundalis?
For a last few days, some clever people have opened their shops
To mitigate the effect of the eclipse on the people.
And there are queues,
There are prior appointments.
At least the economy of these people will improve,
Irrespective of their own star sign.
Something else will happen in the next 123 years to keep running their
business.
There are lunar eclipses for that matter.

*

Well, the same beggar is still here.
For the last so many years standing in the same pose.
Had he been in Himalayas, he would have been worshipped like a deity.
Standing at the corner of two streets meeting at the signal,
In the same cladding, without changing it any day.
Maybe it is his professional requirement.
Maybe he is having more than a pair of the clothes,

Torn and patched in the same manner by him so as to hide his
financial progress.
In Mumbai some beggars earn more than those who put coins in their pots.

*

Some of his associates, in the half full compartments of the trains
Will be smothering *Rafi, Lata and Kishor,*
One after another with pieces of asbestos in their right hand
As a musical support instruments.
And surprisingly, the passengers will put their hands in the pockets.
It is not yet known whether people give money to stop them
Or pay them for having shaken their nostalgia.
Lata-Rafi Duet for as less as 50 cents or even further less.
Any single page of the *Copyright Act, 1957* must be costlier than this.
Kishor and Rafi are now sitting before their respective Gods.
They are not likely to reborn to die twice.
May God bestow fortitude upon *Lata*
To bear the killings of her immortal songs.
These train singers, in the evening, under the bridge of the railway stations,
Escaping from the eyes of the police,
Will push their plights in the rings of the smoke,
Inhaled by them from the silver colored foils held above the candles.
The alien like poor children of the no Gods
Will then sleep under the bridge until a policeman hits on their coccyx,
Sometime around midnight.
We call it dawn.
The city never sleeps.
It will go around like this.
Incessantly.
For uncountable days—in fact nights.
The poor guys of my sorts
Who drown biscuits in the tea and eat
Will not be able to do anything
despite I feel I was of the similar age once

And remember the dearth.
I can not hear their cries.
I have developed extraordinary filter
In the auditory canal of my hearing sense organ.
It does not allow the screams to enter the portion in the brain
Capable of analyzing the trauma wrapped in the sound waves.
How and why will I hear others when I am not heard of.
So many sounds, so many voices, so many noises.
A vernacular cacophony filled in the atmosphere of the city.
Perhaps all this will come to an end
After a few years when the sun will break into pieces
Due to its own temperature.
Until then probably there are no chances of any change.
The crows will remain black either till then
Except a few like me who are destined white.
Although crow.
Some call it abnormality.
The black crows.

*

Once I had suggested her of our own nest.
EMI payable by me and other provisions payable by her.
Simple as that.
The nest of two awaiting the entry of third.
She told me on my face that the crows build nests.
She wanted to have a far more big house.
Maybe the hallucination effect of the love imagines everything larger
than life.
Sooner of later the delusions follow.
Her expectations are beyond my control and capacities.
Very strenuous to bring anything to her level.
Efforts are on.
The loan is passed and the sanction letter is in the hands.
1 BHK within the city limits may not be distant dream now for me.

550-550 sq ft.

This much space only is remained in this city per normal and capable person.

Anything beyond this is nothing less than building the castles in the air.

Luckily, the sky above my head belongs to me.

*

I believe,
Under the skies,
Before the ocean,
On the banks of river,
In the deep woods,
I am no more than a hypothesis—
Hypothesis of identity
Wrapped in an inverted comma,
Placed in the bracket of existence.

*

The beggar has stretched his hand in the usual manner before me.
I have never given the beggar a single *paisa* before.
But, today is a different day altogether.
I pushed my fingers in the pocket and pulled out a *rupee* coin
And placed in his empty bowl.
He is giving me blessings that the God will give me 10 million rupees
In redemption of 1 Rupee.
All others who give him anything will receive the same blessing.
When? Where and How?
Nobody is going to ask.
Nobody knows.

Everybody anticipates.
Maybe the beggar has the answer
But nobody wants to hear the reality.

*

It is heard that once upon a time,
He used to travel in his own car to the *market*.
It was his dream that he will bend the sensex his way
And the *Jeejibhoy Tower* will stand before him,
Bowed on its base to have a look at him.
Strangely, the same has happened.
He is standing at such a juncture from where the entire *market* looks at him
Bowed on its base,
Mocking at him.

*

1 million for 1 Rupee.
The city must be the cheapest one in the world.
Every *paisa**
redeemable in more than 100 blessings.
Except the boarding and lodging,
Everything is cheap and abundant.
Hate, hatred, honors, salutes, salutations, credits, credentials—everything.
It has chain of retailers for every sort.
With the tags and without the tags.
With the concession and without the concession.
Price varies depending largely upon the time
Just like the shadow in the sun dial.
The size of the shadow inversely proportionate to the time in hours
and minutes.
Same logic applies here.

*

And yet there are options.
Everything and everyone has options.
Options have further options and options and options.
Ultimately, just options are remained
And the options are sometimes taken as originals.
The false said 100 times takes the shape of truth.
In the same manner, the options have killed the originals.
It is difficult to find original in the ocean of options.
Perhaps the originals might have lost their originality
Resulting in loss of their relevance.

*

Bought a red T-shirt and a jeans trousers on the fashion street footpath.
A little preparation for the evening meet.
She likes red.
A print-out of the poems.
A clean shave.
Just a mild perfume is to be added in the evening on the right palm.
Preparation of the magnitude must not have made
Even by my parents at the time of my birth.
In fact they could not have afforded anything.
While making both the ends meet,
They fatigued and exhausted.
Must have lived dreaming that any one of three of us
Would take them out of the dung.
Certainly, we would have.
But they are no more now.
The dung still follows me.
Fortunately enough,
I have managed to maintain a considerable distance from it.
At least till the moment.
However, it is not far away a moment by which it might engulf me.
It is, for the insects of the dung, said that they do not remain there forever.

*

My mother.
She died when I was 19.
The dead woman walking.
She walked taking her legs in the hand.
Somehow.
She knew it better that she won't survive much.
Worked.
Worked
And worked.
And then died,
Leaving behind a compassionate appointment for me in the Office.
Every evening she used look through the window for me to come
home safe.
Her eyes always would search me.
I believe, she is still there around me.
Most of the times, I feel her existence.
She has not died after the death.
I feel her eyes roving through the window from the other side of it.

*

The carved window.
The tinted window.
Single window.
Double window.
Window.
A permeable partition,
Between the two worlds.
I changed it.
So many times.
The other side has remained unchanged.
Yet.
Including my mother.

Let me check how it looks inside.
From the other side of window.
The time has come.
Perhaps I may meet my mother.
Wish I could hail through the window assuring her that her child is not
spoiled,
At least to the extent she was afraid of.
Had she been alive today,
She would have seen that I am on my feet and firm.

*

Had she been alive today she would have bought a *saree* for her,
In token of her acceptance,
Despite the fact that the girls from other castes and religions
Are not so easily acceptable,
Even today,
Even when the man has set his footprints
On the sands and soils of the very important element in the kundali,
The moon.
The moon is no more a moon
As it used to be a few decades before.
Still it finds its place in everybody's life determining his fate and future.
The moon looked like a dot in the limited firmament
Spread 90 degrees on either sides of the nose and me
Like a drop in the celestial sea.

*

Hundred of thousands of drops like me,
Scattered on the lanes, streets and gullies,
Moving in all possible directions like the Brownian Motion,
In search of something.
Sometimes unknown and unwarranted other times.
Everyone has a story to tell, an epic to share.

Everyone is a saga in this city.
All authors hence no audience.
Therefore, every shoulder carries a haunted brain.
Me, the one amongst them.

*

No one knows his destination barring a few
Who have already reached there
And pushed it beyond the reach of anyone else.
They are there in the business of carrying it further.
No goals for the rest of the city.
I too have no target.
I can not have one.
The targets here are so big.
One has to take more than a birth to achieve them.
At least I will not have a grievance
Of not achieving them as I don't have any.
The roses have no objectives.
They just blossom.
Others have a target to create a black rose with golden dots,
Yet to be genetically engineered.

*

Maybe a day will come when the days will change drastically, at least
for me.
Reluctance may be a vice.
But inertia certainly not.
If you can't change the world, don't change yourself.
The world will adjust to your inertia.
It has to.
It has its businesses.
As nothing could be created or destroyed under the sun
It is better not to indulge

In creating unachievable targets and unreachable goals.
Let it be a business to all those who have no other business.
I want to rest in peace after the last breath.

*

One pyre is being put on another.
The ashes are mixed.
The bones have lost identity.
How will I separate myself,
From the others,
When my turn comes to leave the land?
The graves are full.
Coffins are being piled,
Each one, on many underneath.
How will I rest in peace,
Confined and eternal,
When my turn comes to leave the land?

*

I fail to understand holding the hearts in the hands
Why everyone is running to reach the unknown lands?
Nothing more is required than a piece under the surface
Equal to the distance between the tips of middle fingers of stretched hands.

*

I just need her.
I know if she comes,
The withered roses are not going to rejuvenate,
Neither the sun is not going to remain in the sky forever.
If she doesn't,
The stars will not scatter.
Neither the moon will fall

If she doesn't love me any more and at all.
The tulips will not wither,
The daffodil will not bemoan
If she doesn't love me any more and at all.
The dew will not dry,
The breeze will not freeze
If she doesn't love me any more and at all.
The autumn will not go,
The winter will not cease
If she doesn't love me any more and at all.
The poles will not meet,
The earth will not stop.
If she doesn't love me any more and at all.
The sun will not blacken,
The skies will not flop
If she doesn't love me any more and at all.

*

There is something between the heart and the brain
Which is bringing distorted thoughts.
The parabolas and the hyperbolas of the thoughts
Moving me like a paper ship
In the gusty streams,
Wobbling in all possible directions,
Driven by the external forces,
Marching towards unknown shores,
Uncertain to reach.
But I am not a paper ship.
At least.

*

Yet there remains a question there.
What am I?
What am I?
A part of the planet?
An inhabitant of the universe?
A particle in the galaxy?
What am I?
A soul within the body?
A body with a spirit?
A spirit with a force?
What am I?
A life that lives?
Or a life
Given birth by an agile sperm?
What am I?

*

Why does everyone carry a question mark
On the face in this city of sorrows?
Myself included.
There is grief, there is agony, there is pain,
Yet there is tomorrow.
Myself excluded.

*

The sun never sets here.
It is one more day pushed forward until the suns rises next.
At least for me and the likes.

*

Till the date the destiny is dictating the terms.
A day will come when I will write my future on the face of destiny,
Irrespective of the linear array on my palms.
I will prove that the lines on the palm do not decide the fate.
Otherwise, everyone would have changed them.
It is yet to the discovered whether anything connects
The lines on the palms,
The psalms
And the three monkeys of the *Mahatma.*
The coexistence of all these has no correlation,
Just like the soul which has nothing to do with the heart and the brain.
Both of them stop functioning
At least once in the lifetime of everyone.
Yet the soul remain functional and alive,
For taking us to the next birth
Carrying forward all the sins and virtues of the present birth,
With or without changing the DNA.
Gods know who I was in the last birth and what could be my next
incarnation.
As far as the present form is concerned,
It appears that I must have been on some other planet
Where the definitions are different.

*

It is 2 pm now.
Strolling on the buffer wall of the roaring sea near the *Haji Ali*,
Have prayed standing in front of the *Dargah*.
One more of my God is left.
My own God.
The Ganapati.
The Christ is already inscribed on the hand.

*

I have taken the bus which will take me to His temple in *Prabhadevi*.
Fortunately, I can pray sitting in the bus.
Almost ninety percent people do the same.
And there are many a options as well.
Some of the Gods are hanged on the stems of trees.
Some are firmly placed under the tress
And a few are finding their shelter in the makeshift mandirs,
All scattered across the length and the breadth of the city.
Trauma, grievances, dreams, desires, dearth, plight.
Everyone is placed at the disposal of them
But has no tools to deal with.
Then there is a need of Gods.
The number of Gods extended
In proportion to the requirements and the magnitude.

*

It could have been a little faster to reach by train.
The sensex is down today.
So are the trains likely to be half empty.
The roads will also ply free today.
The bars will be full.
One building decides the movement of the city

And the number of people with or without broken sleeps.
No two consecutive days are alike for everyone here.
Mutability runs in the arteries and veins of the city and almost every resident.

*

I tried changing myself.
But sticking hard to my principle of inertia,
I could not change.
I have not deleted her from the memories.
I have not forgotten her.
I have not distracted myself.
I am still standing on my feet like the mountain
Withstanding the storms and snow
By taking them in the stride.
I am still walking on the streets
Full of thorns and stones,
Carving my way towards her
Despite all the plight.
I am still trying to change
The way I behaved
By setting myself straight
And replacing wrongs by right.

*

Will she come?
More than a thousand times
I have repeated the question to myself.
I have no answer.
She has the answer.
She is the answer.
I am slightly worried.

*

The bus has halted at the depot.
I have alighted and walking to the beach.
The rendezvous.
Once used to be exclusively for us.
The sun is retiring for the day.
The anticipations and the emotions are rising.
All wishes and wills held together against an entry.
Her entry.
No other desires.
No other aspirations.
She and nothing less or nothing more.

*

The whole of life accumulated around a moving dot coming towards
me.
The dot,
The life.
The dot,
A small circle.
Small circles,
Big circles,
Crenate circles,
Thin circles,
Thick circles.
I got them all before,
Either of these at a time.
Or,
All of these, sometimes.
When segregated them all,
I entered into a bigger circle.
Seemingly, the extended circumference of me-
The dot,

With entire paraphernalia embedded within.
Me, the dot awaiting another dot
To merge into me and desirous of remaining merged
For the rest of the life,
Inseparably.

*

The sun has crossed the horizon
And entered into the lives on the other half of the globe.
In the quest for love
I have traveled too long.
And reached the other side of the heart,
Exactly opposite the point
From where I started,
Which leads to the *pila house.*
Fortunately,
The feet are still on the ground.
Distance has not inverted me.
Difference has not inverted me.
Luster has not shaken me.
I am not driven away,
Yet.
The quest will continue till I remain unchanged
Whether or not she meets me.

*

The dot, instead of coming to me has taken a left turn.
Maybe it has another dot waiting for it.
Lucky dots.
Where is mine?

*

The dusk has fallen all over the sands
Turning it into sprinkle of gold.
The nature has set a perfect set.
The sky is yet a little reddish.
Ample to read her eyes.

*

Wait will be over soon.
Soon there will be beginning of unending end.
The heart is pounding in haphazard manner.
The droplets of the sweat are encircling the face.
One more dot is coming towards me.
Is it she?
The dot has stopped and dropped on the sands.
It is not she.
She knows the point.
She knows where we last met.

*

I do not remember
When the last I touched her.
But I remember
She kissed me for the last time.
I do not remember
When the last we spoke.
But I remember
She whispered something for the last time.
I do not remember
When the last I dreamt her.
I do not remember
When the last she loved me.
But I love her unto this moment.

*

The dusk is gone and the dark is prevailing over the sands,
The sea and the entire firmament.
Time is passing fast.
The hours have passed like minutes and the minutes like moments.
She has not come yet.
Policemen have had their stroll.
Having taken their share they have let the pairs engage themselves
Into their business.
The business of love.
For both the classes.
Eunuchs have also snatched their share,
Blessed those who have given them something
And raised their sarees against those who have not.
Once I had also fallen prey to their heinous act.
Since then I am under constant fear psychosis
As and when the fraternity is around me.
It is said to be a good omen when the eunuchs dance on the birth of a child.
I wonder as to why these people of no sex put their credentials to the peril,
Dancing before the people with sex, in a shameful manner.

*

It has been ten by now.
I don't think she will come.
Neither it looks possible.
She must have made up her mind not to meet me again.
Why did she asked me to meet then?
Was it a real call
Or the hallucination of being called?

*

Two years since we last met.
Hundreds of thousands of permutations and combinations
With multiple options must have come across her.
She might have chosen a better alternative.
I must have been imagined to be a dew drop on the pinnacle by her,
Prone to scroll down at a slightest waft.
It is true.
I am a dew drop on the pinnacle.
Sparkling and bright throughout.
And yes,
I am a paradox in the orthodox world of parabolas and the hyperbolas
Filled with eccentric conventions and equations called relationships.
No one can understand me.
Neither she, nor anybody else.

*

I think I must get up now,
Remove the sands on the pant and in the shoes and move towards my
paraphernalia.
The roads will take me
Everywhere,
Somewhere,
Nowhere,
Except to her.

*

I have to forget all the ecstasies and elations, a common heart has.
I have to become uncommon now,
All of a sudden.
Started feeling deserted one like the cacti.
Everyone likes it but nobody takes it home.

The cacti are beautiful
Though they are thorny,
They blossom
And fill the desert with fragrance.
Suns and sands have failed to extinct them.
In fact,
The deserts are known by the cactus.

*

It is likely to rain now.
Oh dear cloud,
Full of water and life,
Please do not shower here
For there is no use
Watering the soil here
As I may not enjoy
The fragrance of flowers.
It is of no use to me.
I have crossed the ecstasies
And elations,
All.
Please go to the distances
In search of the dear departed in uncommon way
And fertile the land of her,
Fill her vicinity with life.
She might see my reflection in something
And remember me for a moment.
And
Might feel that there is someone
In the distant deserts waiting for her to come back
And fill his life by her showers of love.

*

After deducting
Seconds,
Minutes,
Hours
Rendered for the rest of the world,
From every single day,
Hardly any moment was left
To live one day.
Now the time has come to live for the self.
There is no option left either.
I have to live for myself now.
May be the lights will spread
All over again.
The dark of sorrows
Will be over again.
Though the dusk has fallen.
I will not close the eyes.
I will toil through the night.
And,
Wait until dawn.
The lights will spread
All over again.
I will wait until dawn.

*

I have returned to the house without the heart.
The heart might have entangled somewhere in the sands of the beach.
I have thrown it into the sea.

*

Who is there at the niche below the staircase?
A hand of the shadow is emanated from the wall.
The face is not visible.
The shadow is moving in an unusual manner.
Perhaps, someone has come out of the hallucination,
In the same way as that of me with eyes wide open.

*

Nothing is left to be said,
Nothing is left to be done,
Nothing is left to be admired,
Nothing is left to be given.
It is determined.
We will not meet again,
For anything and for any reason.

*

Nothing is to be redeemed.
Nothing is left to be seen.
Nothing is to be trashed
And thrown in the bin.

We will not meet again,
For anything
And for any reason.
The moon is dull.
The stars have gone.
The sky is gloomy
And the life forlorn.
Is there anything
Which shall bring us
Together again?
We will not meet again,
For anything
And for any reason,
Once again to share the
Same pain,
By me alone.

*

Tomorrow, there will be another tomorrow.
For you and me as well.
It is true
That I love her.
I will keep loving
Until the doomsday.
And write her name
On the remainder clay.
The truth is that
She never liked me.
Still I will keep
Bending on my knee.

*

All the equations were solved
But the answers never matched.
It appears that my equation of love
Was not in consonance with the outcome.

*

The time has come to stretch the *chadar* over the face again and look to
the skies Through the same hole wishing no star falls tonight.
But, I will ask her on my way back as to why she is sitting
On the stairway to the heaven?
Who has thrown her there?
Because,
I have forgiven her for all her rude and unbelievable behavior,
As I understood that I was romancing a solid rock made of magma,
Having no heart, No passions, no emotions, no arousals, no instincts
And
No character.

*

The love lost can not destructed me,
Mine
And
Myself.
Still I can invert the mountains,
Squeeze the oceans,
Bend the rainbows,
And pull the stars in the stride including the moon.

I will engage myself in the pursuit of making a black rose with golden dots
To gift her in token of my love,
Perhaps with a view to show her that there was still something to be done.
And that I have done it.
It is midnight again.
I must sleep now to dream anew.

I dedicate this compilation to all who fail to succeed in love with a view to encourage them living second life—without love, despite my belief that love is the most beautiful gift of God, for which I am ready to die twice. However, it is the life, it is the life, it is the life.

My other works are:

quartets on life

The life is the biggest, greatest and most marvelous gift bestowed upon each and everyone on this third planet from the sun. May be there is life on other rocks as well and mankind there may have or may not have the similar emotions, feelings and behavioral patterns as that of us. Taking into account the span since the first creature breathed till date or from the time of the big bang till the moment, hardly any fraction of a moment one gets to live his own life. Still he lives—sometimes trying to live for himself and most of times for the others. Any single life is bigger than any canvas, any novel, any tale. It can not be dovetailed in any form of prose of poetry. However, an effort is made in identifying the life in the mirror of quartets— a form of miniature poetry.

The quartets in this compilation are rendered to various aspects of life like love, passion, emotions, dearth, plight and so on and so forth. Real life experiences have been given shape of quartets (a four line poem form) decorated with the words. These quartets are the feelings, emotions and the unknown eruptions of something from the inner core of the heart which tries to come out every alternate moment but could not succeed due to intrinsic coercions. The quartets have come out as natural reactions to world around, the responses to the pathetic behaviors of others and the inner feelings in response thereto.

Infinity

It is a short novel depicting the battle of a young man against all the odds he faces in his life. It is journey of the young man from nowhere to somewhere and beyond elucidating the real life dilemmas and dearth and capacity of an ordinary man to deal with them. The novel is being published shortly.

Glossary
(in the order of appearance of words)

Kundali
(array or position of stars and planet at the time of birth, tabulated in a chart)
Taj
(Greatest monument built by Shahjehan in memory of his love.)
BHK
(short form for Bedroom Hall Kitchen—a term used in Mumbai for describing apartments)
wada-pav
(a famous snack of Mumbai consisting of potatoes dipped in gram flour and fried, served with bread)
8.57 CCG fast
(a fast local starting from Borivali leading to Churchgate on western railway in Mumbai)
9.10 CCG fast
(a fast local starting from Borivali leading to Churchgate on western railway in Mumbai)
nallahs
(gutters)
EMIs
(equated monthly installments of loans etc.)
pind dan
(a ritual performed after the death)
pind
(a symptomatic word for body, used in the rites after death)

13th?
(13th day after the death when pind dan is performed)
mithi river
(a river in Mumbai)
Mahim creek
(a creek of Arabian Sea in Mumbai)
26th July
(day on which heavy downpours flooded Mumbai in 2005)
MCGM
(short form for Municipal Corporation of Greater Mumbai)
Dadar
(a suburban station in Mumbai)
Mandir
(temple)
Masjid
(mosque)
Sensex
(index of Mumbai Stock Market)
Arabian Sea
(sea on the western coast of India)
Mc'donald's
(famous chain of international restaurant)
bhajan mandalis
(group of people singing holy songs)
Shirdiwale Sai Baba
(one of the greatest deities)
Bhajans
(holy songs praising the Gods)
Darbar
(Place of worshipping)
Ayodhya
(birthplace of Lord Rama)
Shirdi
(a place in Maharashtra where there is main temple of Sai Baba)

auto
(auto rickshaw)
Samrat
(a theatre in western suburb of Mumbai)
dance bar
(beer bars with the arrangements of dance and music)
.Mt. Merry Church
(a famous church in Mumbai located in Bandra)
Gutka
(a preparation of tobacco which larger section of people chew and spit)
Sachin
(Sachin Tendulkar—the all time great cricketer of India)
Paise
(100th part of one Indian rupee)
Rani Baug
(a zoo in Mumbai)
Khajuraho
(a place of Hindu and Jain temples famous for it erotic sculptures)
26th November
(the day on which terrorists from Pakistan attacked Mumbai)
.33 crore Gods
(the number of Gods as per the Hindu belief)
market
(a general term used for share market)
Lord Ganapati
(one of the greatest Gods of Hindus having elephant's head)
Rafi
(Indian playback singing maestro)
Lata
(Indian playback singing maestro)
Kishor
(Indian playback singing maestro)
Jeejibhoy Tower
(office of Mumbai Stock Exchange)

Saree
(an Indian female garment having unstitched cloth ranging from 4 to 9 metres in length)
Mahatma
(Mahatma Gandhi)
Haji Ali
(a mosque and tomb located on an islet off the coast of Mumbai)
Dargah
(tomb)
Prabhadevi
(a place in Mumbai where there is temple of Lord Ganapati)
pila house
(a general term used in Mumbai for red light area in southern Mumbai)
chadar
(an Indian form of quilt)

Lightning Source UK Ltd.
Milton Keynes UK
03 January 2011

165117UK00002B/287/P